The Adventures of Scuba Jack
Copyright 2021 by Beth Costanzo
All rights reserved

Zebras are one of nature's coolest looking creatures! There are three different types of zebras: the **plains zebra**, **Grevy's zebra** and **mountain zebra**. All three zebras live in Africa. A Zebra's skin is actually black with a white "coat".

Each Zebra has its own unique pattern of stripes, just like humans have their own unique fingerprints. Scientists think this may help Zebras recognize each other or for camouflage. Their stripey coat gets rid of 70% of incoming heat so they don't overheat in the African sun.

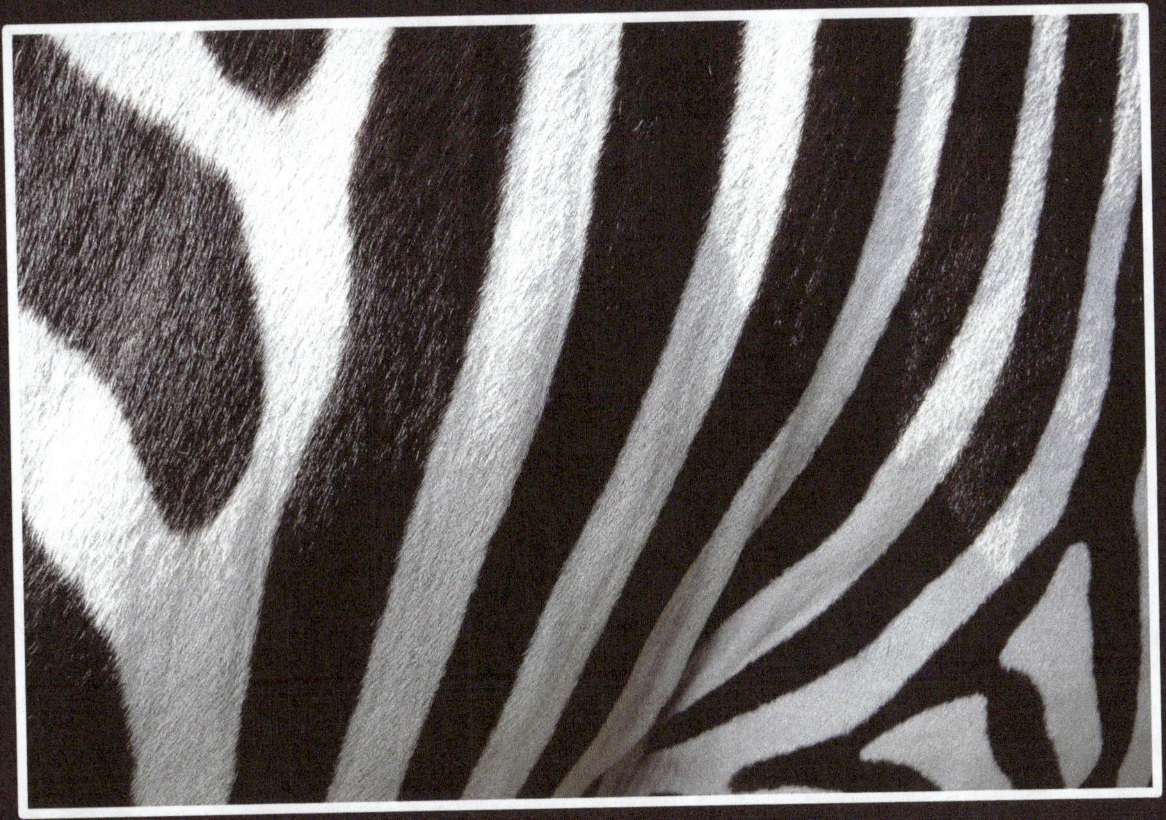

The Adventures of SCUBA JACK

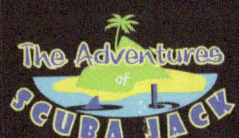

Zebras tend to stay in large groups called herds. Within herds, Zebras stay in smaller family groups. Zebras are herbivores, an animal that eats plants, so herds are always trying to find fresh grass and water.

Sometimes zebras will nibble leaves from bushes, shrubs, twigs and bark. Their teeth are well adapted for this, with sharp incisors at the front of their mouth to bite the grass, and large molars at the back for crushing and grinding. They will travel long distances to find new feeding grounds during the dry seasons.

Zebras live up to 25 years in the wild. Zebras are very closely related to horses and donkeys. Their top speed is 40 mph. Zebras have great hearing and eyesight, which helps them stay clear of predators such as lions, leopards, hyenas, and cheetahs. Zebras can be very aggressive animals with their piercing bites and powerful kicks that can cause serious damage and even kill these predators. If Zebras feel threatened, they will form a semi-circle facing the attacker and prepare to fight. If a Zebra is hurt, other zebras will circle around and try to make the predator go away. They refuse to leave their family behind!

Zebra QUIZ

Write the correct answer in the box

Where do Zebras live?

1- Australia

2- Africa

3- South America

Write the correct answer in the box

What type of animal is a zebra?

1- Omnivore

2- Carnivore

3- Herbivore

Write the correct answer in the box

What are Zebras fierce fighting skills?

1- Squeezing

2- Biting and kicking

3- Poisoning

Write the correct answer in the box

How fast can a zebra run?

1- 40 mph

2- 30 mph

3- 50mph

Zebra Activities

Trace then rewrite the phrase below.

Z for Zebra

Count the zebras then circle the answer.

5 6 7	5 6 7
7 9 8	7 9 8

Maze

Help the Zebra to find its way

Zebra Craft

- Cut out the Zebra parts
- Glue them together
- Draw the stripes on the zebra
- Have fun!

Visit us at:

www.adventuresofscubajack.com